soul care
for the battle

Books by Susie Larson

soul care
for the battle

A Guided Journal

SUSIE LARSON

BETHANYHOUSE

a division of Baker Publishing Group
Minneapolis, Minnesota

© 2022 by Susie Larson

Published by Bethany House Publishers
11400 Hampshire Avenue South
Minneapolis, Minnesota 55438
www.bethanyhouse.com

Bethany House Publishers is a division of
Baker Publishing Group, Grand Rapids, Michigan

Printed in the United States of America

ISBN 978-0-7642-4143-7 (paper)
ISBN 978-1-4934-4101-3 (ebook)

Cover design by Emily Weigel

Author represented by The Steve Laube Agency

Baker Publishing Group publications use paper produced from sustainable forestry practices and post-consumer waste whenever possible.

22 23 24 25 26 27 28   7 6 5 4 3 2 1

INTRODUCTION

Tend to your soul in every season of life. Especially in times of trial.

Dear Fellow Warrior,

I'm genuinely honored to travel this journey with you. If you've picked up this journal, it likely means you're walking through a difficult time. So sorry about that. You may know this already, but I'll say it anyway: *God is the strength of your heart, and He has no intention of letting you lose this battle. You might get knocked down. You might forget who you are on occasion. You might even forget who God is, but He'll never forget you. He won't look away, lose your address, or fail to care. He's deeply and profoundly invested in your journey. He cares about your heart. He knows about your enemy. And if you'll dare to trust Him, He'll take what the enemy meant for evil and turn it for good. You can trust Him.*

The purpose of this journal is to help you consistently care for your soul in the days ahead. When the storms rage, the first thing to go is our sense of direction. We are anchored to a good God, and when we regularly make time to take inventory of our thoughts, to rehearse His promises, and to make room for laughter, we'll fare much better in the long run.

I originally wrote this journal in conjunction with my book *Strong in Battle: Why the Humble Will Prevail*; however, don't feel obligated to purchase the book. ☺ It's an intense handbook on how to stand in battle. *Soul Care for the Battle* was written to help you think redemptively, find reasons for thanksgiving, and go deeper in your prayers. No matter what your situation, it's my prayer that as you work your way through these pages, you'll remember that you're not alone. In fact, you're in excellent hands. God is with you. He's got you. Let's get started.

How to Use This Journal

I've journaled for my whole adult life. And the one rule that has helped me stay consistent in recording my thoughts and prayers for decades is this: *There are no rules.*

So that's our rule! *No rules.*

I purposely didn't label these entries by days or weeks. You may feel the need to immerse yourself in reflection on a particular day. You'll likely work your way through five to ten of the exercises. On certain days, you might want to sit with one practice and consider it more deeply than I'm asking of you here. Other days, you might want to reread what you've already written. (I often do that with my journals, and I always marvel at the consistent ways God has spoken to me.) If you're that kind of processor, it might be an excellent idea for you to purchase a blank notebook to accompany you on this journey.

You'll notice that specific exercises repeat throughout the journey. That's on purpose. We all tend to heal in layers—one memory, experience, and belief at a time. As you walk intimately with God and learn to trust His love for you, He'll likely bring to mind things you'd long forgotten, experiences He wants to help you reframe. And, as you journey upward and onward, you'll make a few missteps along the way. When you draw near to God with honesty, you'll find Him full of love and mercy. His grace abounds toward you. Our conversations with God—especially during trying times—are of utmost importance in our spiritual pilgrimage. I want you to have a space to sort through your experiences. I pray this journal provides that for you.

Take your time.

Invite God to make Himself known to you in tangible ways.

Trust Him to speak to you and through you.

Don't rush.

Just rest, reflect, and record what springs up from your heart.

I'll be praying for you.

With much love and affection,
Susie Larson

How we view our *trials* when we're in them and what we tell ourselves about them on the other side directly impacts the kind of *warrior* we become.

—*Strong in Battle*, p. 85

Pray the Scripture

Lord Jesus,

Teach me how to live, O Lord. I trust You to lead me along the right path, for my enemy has me in his crosshairs. Stretch out Your hand against him and rescue me. I hide myself in You! Even though I'm fighting a battle right now, I believe with all my heart that I will see Your goodness in the land of the living. I will see Your promises come true. Help me to be brave, confident, and courageous as I patiently wait for You. Amen.

Psalm 27:11–14, paraphrased and personalized

From Where I Stand

Current Battles

- Most pressing: ....
  ....
  ....

- Most concerning: ....
  ....
  ....

- Background noise but bothersome: ....
  ....
  ....

Faith Perspective in This Moment

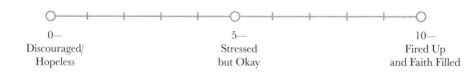

0—	5—	10—
Discouraged/	Stressed	Fired Up
Hopeless	but Okay	and Faith Filled

Thoughts I Have on Repeat

I'm Listening, Lord

When I quiet my heart, here's what I sense God saying to me . . .

The God who put the *stars* in place delights in every detail of your life.

He is fierce in your defense. He tempers your *storm*, so you'll come through it more grounded in Him than you ever imagined. You can *trust* Him.

———

—*Strong in Battle*, p. 13

Pray the Scripture

Write out this passage in a personalized and prayerful way.

Hear my cry, O God;
*   listen to my prayer.*

From the ends of the earth I call to you,
*   I call as my heart grows faint;*
*   lead me to the rock that is higher than I.*
For you have been my refuge,
*   a strong tower against the foe.*

Psalm 61:1–3 NIV

Holy Lament

Truly holy lament is a sacred practice in which we allow our heartbreak to move us toward God and not away from Him. We cry out to the God who listens, cares deeply, and is infinitely able to redeem our story. And we believe that He'll do something about that heartbreak. Holy lament allows us to miraculously open ourselves to the life-giving influence of almighty God while we travel the dirt roads of grief, heartache, and loss.

Self-Pity

On the other hand, self-pity drains the life out of us, and all that is beautiful in our lives. While obsessing over our disappointments, we miss the eternal opportunities all around us. Take some time to sort through your hardships in a way that disposes of self-pity and leaves you with the holy invitation to enter the healing practice of lament. Write down your thoughts.

Holy Lament

Write out your prayer of lament to God.

Things I Love about My Life

Blessings in My Battle

Sincere gratitude awakens a physiological response in our body. It's also healing for the soul. Though it feels impossible to thank God *for* most of our battles, it's quite possible to find reasons to thank Him *in* our battle. Imagine taking your burdens and spreading them all over your dinner table. Can you find any treasures there? Anything for which you're sincerely grateful? Do you see God at work? Do you now know something about God or even yourself that you didn't know before? Name some of the blessings in your battle.

Blessings in My Battle

🔥
🔥
🔥
🔥
🔥
🔥
🔥
🔥
🔥
🔥
🔥
🔥
🔥
🔥

Taking Thoughts Captive

For though we walk in the *flesh*, we do not war according to the flesh. For the *weapons* of our warfare are not carnal but mighty in God for pulling down strongholds, casting down arguments and every high thing that *exalts* itself against the knowledge of God, bringing every thought into *captivity* to the obedience of Christ.

—2 Corinthians 10:3–5 NKJV

Thoughts That Don't Belong in My Brain

The enemy's strategy is to flood our thoughts with visions of all that is wrong in this broken, fallen world to the point we don't even think to look for the positive anymore. Cynicism just becomes the way we think, and we don't even notice.

—Jennie Allen, *Get Out of Your Head*[1]

Thoughts about God

We're strong in battle when we remember that
we're tethered to a strong and good God.

Today, I praise You because You are . . .

....

....

....

....

....

....

Today, I'm grateful for . . .

....

....

....

....

....

....

A Faith Perspective

If we look to this life to fulfill all our promised joy and happiness and for our story to tie up into a nice bow, we will live perpetually disappointed. But if we expect to face a few battles on the journey, knowing that God will redeem all things, we might find the courage and holy optimism our souls need. What if we learned to grow comfortable in the tension of the now and the not yet? Might our eyes open to the perpetual beauty and promise all around us? There is a day coming when Jesus will wipe away our tears, heal our broken hearts and our broken bodies. He'll make the wrong things right and reveal to the whole world that we belong to Him. He'll deal with the devil in the way that he deserves. But until then, we will feel—at the same time and sometimes even in the exact moment—both sadness and gladness, hope and despair. So how do we keep an eternal perspective in the here and now? For one, we get good at remembering.

We get good at remembering . . .

I Have Seen His Goodness

His goodness . . .

His beauty . . .

His provision . . .

His intervention . . .

> Faith is something that looks backward—we remember the ways God has come through for his people, and for us, and our belief is strengthened that he will come through again.
>
> —John Eldredge, *All Things New*[2]

Reflective Questions / Journal Prompts

How has this battle taken a toll on my soul?

In what ways have I neglected self-care?

What can I do today to nourish my soul?

Healthy Choices I Made Today

Every step toward healing and wholeness matters.

Have you not known?
Have you not heard?
The everlasting God, the LORD,
The Creator of the ends of the earth,
Neither faints nor is weary.
His understanding is unsearchable.
He gives power to the weak,
And to those who have no might He increases
strength.
Even the youths shall faint and be weary,
And the young men shall utterly fall,
But those who wait on the LORD
Shall renew their strength;
They shall mount up with wings like
eagles,
They shall run and not be weary,
They shall walk and not faint.

Isaiah 40:28–31 NKJV, emphasis added

Space for Reflection

I am going to be okay.

Space for Reflection

I am going to be okay.

Move your piles out of sight.
Create some space where
you can *breathe*.
Turn off your screens.
Put on your favorite worship *playlist*

AND *dance*.

Fully Alive Moment

Write about a time when you were most fully alive,
when you felt like the best version of yourself.

Fully Alive Moment

Write about a time when you were most fully alive,
when you felt like the best version of yourself.

_____

_____

_____

_____

_____

_____

_____

_____

_____

_____

Grace to you and peace from God our Father and the Lord
Jesus Christ.
  I thank my God upon every remembrance of you.

Philippians 1:2–3 NKJV

Read through your written memory and
answer the following questions.

Precious Memories . . .

What were you wearing? What might that outfit say about you?

What about that memory made you happy?

What senses were most awakened in that memory (e.g., what you tasted, touched, felt, heard, or saw)?

Often, the more we *heal*,
the easier it is to remember
our *good* memories.
May God continue His *beautiful*,
important,
soul-stirring
healing process
in your life.

Precious Memories . . .

What does this memory say about you?

_____

_____

_____

_____

_____

_____

How is this memory speaking to you even now?

_____

_____

_____

_____

_____

_____

_____

Precious Memories . . .

What in this memory offers you insights into the ways God wants to restore you? With the framework of this memory in mind, write down what restoration might look like for you.

Take a moment and thank God for the nuances of this precious memory He has given you.

Our *memories* and *experiences*
are clay, stone, and oil pastels
that the Spirit of God
longs to *shape* within us
as something beautiful.

———

—Casey Tygrett, *As I Recall*[3]

Pray the Scripture

Write out this passage in a personalized and prayerful way.

All praise to God, the Father of our Lord Jesus Christ, who has blessed us with every spiritual blessing in the heavenly realms because we are united with Christ.

Ephesians 1:3

Make a Memory This Week . . .

Did you know that anticipating good things is nourishing for your brain and very healing to your body?

Some fun things I could do this week . . .

_____

_____

_____

_____

My plan . . .

_____

_____

_____

_____

Why I look forward to this event . . .

_____

_____

_____

_____

Things I Love about My Life

Expectations versus Expectancy

Often, we opt not to look forward with expectancy because we don't want to be disappointed. It's true that our plans don't always turn out as we'd hoped. But the very nature of holy anticipation is what our souls desperately need. There's a big difference between rigid expectations and holy expectancy. My mentor once told me that expectation is premeditated disappointment. But holy expectancy is living with wide-eyed wonder, open hands, and a heart that believes that any day now, God might break through.

Expectations versus Expectancy

Think of a time when you knew you were white-knuckling rigid expectations. What was the outcome?

Expectations versus Expectancy

Identify a time when you dared to hope and dream a little, but with a heart yielded to God's ultimate plans. What was the outcome?

_____

_____

_____

_____

_____

_____

_____

_____

_____

_____

_____

_____

> "The Lord is my portion," says my soul,
> "Therefore I hope in Him!"
>
> Lamentations 3:24 NKJV

The Memories I Made This Week

Memories I made this week that I didn't expect . . .

_____

_____

_____

_____

Memories I made that I intentionally pursued . . .

_____

_____

_____

_____

Ways I'm growing when it comes to expectations versus expectancy . . .

_____

_____

_____

_____

Memories I'll Make Someday

Finish this sentence as many times as you'd
like and expand on it a bit.

Someday, I'd really like to . . .

Pray the Scripture

Lord Jesus,

I declare by faith that I am filled with joy because I trust in You! My strength comes from You. I have fixed my eyes on You, and my heart is set on eternity. Even when I walk through the valley of weeping, it becomes a place of refreshing springs because You are there with me. In every season, I will see Your faithfulness, and I will continue to grow stronger (not weaker) until I appear before You on that great day when I get to see You face to face. Until then, I'll keep marching, keep believing, and keep trusting that You're with me every step of the way. Thank you, Lord. In Your precious name I pray, Amen.

Psalm 84:5–7, paraphrased and personalized

Soul Care for the Battle

From Where I Stand

Current Battles

- Most pressing: ....
  ....
  ....

- Most concerning: ....
  ....
  ....

- Background noise but bothersome: ....
  ....
  ....

Faith Perspective in This Moment

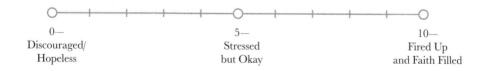

0—	5—	10—
Discouraged/	Stressed	Fired Up
Hopeless	but Okay	and Faith Filled

Thoughts I Have on Repeat

I'm Listening, Lord

When I quiet my heart, here's what I sense God saying to me . . .

I'm Listening, Lord

When I quiet my heart, here's what I sense God saying to me . . .

Soul Care for the Battle

No matter where your fear and anxiety come from, Jesus *cares deeply* about your battle fatigue. He not only *recognizes* the reality of your battle, but He is also moved with *compassion* to help you move to a better place than you may find yourself in right now.

—*Strong in Battle*, pp. 22–23

Holy Lament

Hear my prayer, O LORD,
and let my cry come to You.
Do not hide Your face from me in the day of my trouble;
Incline Your ear to me;
in the day that I call, answer me speedily.

Psalm 102:1–2 NKJV

Be honest with God
about the hurts in your heart.
He is filled with compassion
and abounding in love.
He wants a real, authentic, honest
relationship with you.
You'll find Him to be an amazing Father
and a wonderful Friend.
He will heal your hurts,
restore your soul,
defend your honor,
and make you whole.
You can trust Him.
He'll see you through
to the other side of this trial.

Holy Lament

Write out your prayer of lament to God.

Holy Lament

Write out your prayer of lament to God.

Things I Love about My Life

Blessings in My Battle

Taking Thoughts Captive

And so, dear brothers and sisters, I plead with you to *give* your bodies to God because of all he has done for you. Let them be a *living* and holy sacrifice—the kind he will find acceptable. This is truly the way to *worship* him. Don't copy the behavior and customs of this world, but let God *transform* you into a new person by changing the way you think. Then you will learn to know God's will for you, which is *good* and pleasing and perfect.

Romans 12:1–2

When a *harmful* thought or
temptation comes into our minds,
we have a *choice*.
We can either discard that
thought or entertain it.
If we discard it, good.
But if we *entertain* it, that's
when the Devil sits at our table.

———

—Louie Giglio, *Don't Give the Enemy
a Seat at Your Table*[4]

Thoughts That Don't Belong in My Brain

Thoughts about God

*We're strong in battle when we remember that
we're tethered to a strong and good God.*

Today, I praise You because You are . . .

_____

_____

_____

_____

_____

_____

Today, I'm grateful for . . .

_____

_____

_____

_____

_____

_____

_____

A Faith Perspective

God turns broken stories into beautiful prose and unwanted pages into stunning narratives of victory.

—Sharon Jaynes, *When You Don't Like Your Story*[5]

In my book *Fully Alive: Learning to Flourish—Mind, Body & Spirit*, I wrote,

> *"The storms reveal the lies we believe*
> *and the truths we need."*[6]

You have certain events from your past that you remember partially, others that you remember vividly, and still others that you remember incorrectly. Another thing to consider is your interpretation of those memories. The door may have slammed in your face, and though you were hurt by man's rejection, you were preserved by God's protection. Sit with this idea for a bit. Ask God to bring to the surface a memory that He wants to rescript. *Lord, show me the lies I've believed and the truths I need.*

....

....

....

....

....

Important Memories

I remember a time when . . .

Important Memories

I remember a time when . . .

Important Memories

What does this memory say *to* you that you sense is not true?

....

....

....

....

What does this memory say *about* you that you sense is not true?

....

....

....

....

What does this memory say *to* you *about* God that is not true?

....

....

....

....

The spiritual practice of remembering—the practice of engaging with God in our *memories*—is refusing to passively receive our story and script up to this point, and instead actively embracing God's *presence* and our humanity in the midst of it.

As adults, we return to our childhood memories and engage with God there. We see the way our *stories* and *scripts* were shaped and humbly say, 'God, help me rewrite what is broken and shortsighted.'

—Casey Tygrett, *As I Recall* [7]

Lord, speak to me. How do You want to
rewrite and redeem my memories?

Lord, speak to me. How do You want to
rewrite and redeem my memories?

Things I Love about My Life

I Have Seen His Goodness

His goodness . . .

His beauty . . .

His provision . . .

His intervention . . .

> Backtrack and remember all the places where God has been so faithful before in your life. And know. Know with the assurance. And boldness. And confidence. He is the same faithful God.
>
> —Lysa TerKeurst[8]

Reflective Questions / Journal Prompts

How has this battle taken a toll on my soul?

In what ways have I neglected self-care?

What can I do today to nourish my soul?

Healthy Choices I Made Today

Every step toward healing and wholeness matters.

The LORD is my shepherd;
I shall not want.
He makes me to lie down in green pastures;
He leads me beside the still waters.
He restores my soul;
He leads me in the paths of righteousness
For His name's sake.

Yea, though I walk through the valley of the shadow
    of death,
I will fear no evil;
For You are with me;
Your rod and Your staff, they comfort me.
You prepare a table before me in the presence of
    my enemies;
You anoint my head with oil;
My cup runs over.
Surely goodness and mercy shall follow me
All the days of my life;
And I will dwell in the house of the Lord
Forever.

Psalm 23 NKJV, emphasis mine

Space for Reflection

I am going to be okay.

Space for Reflection

I am going to be okay.

☐ Go out of your way to behold *beauty* today.

☐ Find a good reason to *smile*.

☐ Whisper a *prayer* of thanks for all that's right in your world.

☐ Put on your favorite *song*

AND *sing* …

Repentance

In my experience, repentance is good for the soul and puts my heart right before God. His heart is always right toward me. But often when I sin, I sense the Holy Spirit wince within me. My natural tendency is to shrivel, shrink back, or pull away, but God always wants me to run toward Him, not away from Him. I know my relationship with God is secure because of what Jesus did on the cross, but I believe that my fellowship with Him is strengthened when I'm honest about my wandering ways. Also, when I'm honest with God, I'm more likely to be honest with others.

Confess your sins to each other and pray for each other so that you may be healed. The earnest prayer of a righteous person has great power and produces wonderful results.

James 5:16

Soul Care for the Battle

Repentance

Lord, forgive me . . .

For these gifts I've taken for granted . . .

For blaming You for my troubles . . .

For my default ways of handling stress . . .

Repentance

Lord, forgive me . . .

For harboring unforgiveness in my heart . . .

....

....

....

....

For the unkind thoughts I've had toward others . . .

....

....

....

....

For the negative ways I've allowed my battles to impact me . . .

....

....

....

....

In every distress or devilish plot set against us, we can *emerge* better for it. It is the redemptive power of Christ reversing the plans of Satan and annulling the effects of *death* in our lives. Although you may be in a place of fear, sin, or emotional defeat, your current condition is not a *limitation* to the Almighty. From where you are, you can *reach* the stronghold of God.

—Francis Frangipane,
The Stronghold of God[9]

Names I Call Myself

Names God Calls Me

You are a chosen people. You are royal priests, a holy nation, God's very own possession. As a result, you can show others the goodness of God, for he called you out of the darkness into his wonderful light.

1 Peter 2:9

A Healed You

Imagine yourself a year from now.
What might a healed you look like?

I Am with You and for You

Do not be afraid, for I have ransomed you.
    I have called you by name; you are mine.
When you go through deep waters,
    I will be with you.
When you go through rivers of difficulty,
    you will not drown.
When you walk through the fire of oppression,
    you will not be burned up;
    the flames will not consume you.
For I am the Lord, your God,
    the Holy One of Israel, your Savior.

Isaiah 43:1–3

I Have Seen His Goodness

He provided . . .

_____

_____

_____

He prevented . . .

_____

_____

_____

He intervened . . .

_____

_____

_____

He delivered . . .

_____

_____

_____

Soul Care for the Battle

The Ways He Loves Me

Pause and ponder the countless ways God has shown
you that He loves you. Write down your thoughts.

Make a Memory This Week . . .

Anticipating good things is nourishment for your brain and very healing to your body.

Some fun things I could do this week . . .

....

....

....

....

My plan . . .

....

....

....

....

Why I look forward to this event . . .

....

....

....

....

The Memories I Made This Week

Memories I made this week that I didn't expect . . .

_____

_____

_____

_____

Memories I made that I intentionally pursued . . .

_____

_____

_____

_____

Ways that I'm growing when it comes to expectations versus expectancy . . .

_____

_____

_____

_____

- ☐ *Call* a friend or family member.
- ☐ Recall a favorite *memory* together.
- ☐ *Laugh* a little louder than seems appropriate. ☺
- ☐ Tell her one thing you *love* about her.
- ☐ *Pray* together before you hang up.
- ☐ Raise your hands in the air and thank God for His *goodness*.

Healthy Choices I Made Today

Every step toward healing and wholeness matters.

Faith Declaration

Which part of this declaration does your soul need most?

As a citizen of the heavenly kingdom,
An heir of God and joint-heir with Christ,
Filled with the Spirit of the Living God,
I SPEAK WITH PRECISION,
I PRAY WITH POWER,
I walk in authority.
I am anointed and appointed,
Blessed and beloved,
Bold and brave,
Called and courageous,
Because I know God is with me.
I will triumph over my enemy,
And I will stand with Jesus on that final day.
—*Strong in Battle*, p. 147

Faith Declaration

Take the statements that most resonated with you from the previous page and write out your own personalized faith declaration. Find some Scripture to support your declaration.

Pray the Scripture

Precious Father,

In Your strength and by the resurrection power of the Holy Spirit within me, I will run this race to win the prize. I've fixed my eyes on Jesus—He's the author and the finisher of my faith! Jesus, to think You had me on Your heart when You endured the cross. Because of Your great love, You defeated sin and death and the devil's claim on my life. I am no victim! I refuse to be discouraged. I embrace the joy of knowing You and I will persevere because of You. I'm running this race to win. I refuse to be distracted. I'm focused, purposeful, and prayerful. Thank you, Lord, for breathing fresh life in me. I receive all You lovingly want to give. In Jesus' matchless name, I pray. Amen.

Hebrews 12:1–3, paraphrased and personalized

From Where I Stand

Current Battles

- Most pressing: ....

....

....

- Most concerning: ....

....

....

- Background noise but bothersome: ....

....

....

Faith Perspective in This Moment

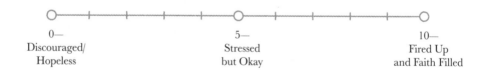

0—
Discouraged/
Hopeless

5—
Stressed
but Okay

10—
Fired Up
and Faith Filled

Thoughts I Have on Repeat (healthy and unhealthy)

Taking Thoughts Captive

Guard your *heart* above
all else, for it determines
the *course* of your life.

Proverbs 4:23

Thoughts That Don't Belong in My Brain

Retraining My Brain

It's time to put a "Road Closed" sign on the unhealthy thought patterns that lead you into the ditch. It's time to create healthy neural pathways. Pick one of these redemptive phrases (or write your own) and write it out several times.

> *If God is for me, who can stand against me?*
> *I have nothing to fear.*
> (See Romans 8:31.)

> *The power of the risen Lord is alive and at work within me!*
> *I am seated with Christ!*
> (See Ephesians 2:6.)

> *God made a masterpiece when He made me!*
> *And He designed me for a unique and powerful purpose.*
> *I can trust Him.*
> (See Ephesians 2:10.)

Soul Care for the Battle

Thoughts That Don't Belong in My Brain

Retraining My Brain

I'm Listening, Lord

When I quiet my heart, here's what I sense God saying to me . . .

Soul Care for the Battle

I'm Listening, Lord

When I quiet my heart, here's what I sense God saying to me . . .

We need you in the Kingdom! And your utter dependence on God **is** your *superpower*. The God who put the stars in place *delights* in every detail of your life. He is fierce in your *defense*. He tempers your storm, so you'll come through it more grounded in Him than you ever *imagined*. You can trust Him.

—*Strong in Battle*, p. 13

What Are You Afraid Of?

Write out your thoughts.

When You Can't Hear What God Is Saying, Remember What He's Already Said

What has the Lord said to you in the past regarding your fears? What promises has He made? What challenges has He issued?

The devil threatens you
In the very way
That you threaten him.
Turn the tables on him.
Get feisty in your faith
And live out your beautiful purpose.

YOU ARE
BRAVE
BOLD
&
BELOVED

Pray the Scripture

Write out this passage in a prayerful, personalized way.

How precious are your thoughts about me, O God.
They cannot be numbered!
I can't even count them;
they outnumber the grains of sand!
And when I wake up,
you are still with me!

Psalm 139:17–18

....

....

....

....

....

....

....

....

....

....

Things I Love about My Life

Enemy Threats and God's Purposes for You

The enemy often takes past fears, stirs up the idea
of worse scenarios, and then tempts you to imagine
a terrible future that God's not in. But no such
scenario exists in the life of the believer; Jesus is
always with you, and He'll never abandon you.
You are gifted, equipped, anointed, and appointed.
God has confirmed this time and time again.
Yet your lingering sense of self-doubt and unbelief gives
the enemy access to your soul that he doesn't deserve.
It's time to shut him down.
It's time to rise up in faith.
It's time to believe what God says about you.

I'm Listening, Lord

When I quiet my heart, here's what I sense God saying to me . . .

I'm Listening, Lord

When I quiet my heart, here's what I sense God saying to me . . .

Pray the Scripture

Write out this passage in a personalized and prayerful way.

For God has not given us a spirit of fear, but of power and of love and of a sound mind.

2 Timothy 1:7 NKJV

Dare to Believe God for More

What if you considered the enemy's threat, turned it around, and pondered the opposite to be true? What if instead of being bullied by the enemy's threats, you were inspired and encouraged by the promises and purposes of God? Give some thought to that now.

Enemy Threat:	God's Purpose and Promise for Me:
....	....
....	....
....	....
....	....
....	....
....	....
....	....
....	....
....	....
....	....
....	....
....	....

Fear Is a Wilderness

Fear is a wilderness and a wasteland. Nothing thrives there. It is relentless and scorching and barren. To rescue us, God promises to do a new thing. To make a new road. The strongly entrenched neural pathway that leads us automatically to fear and worry will be laid waste and a new road (neural pathway) will be created—a road that leads automatically to faith.

—Jennifer Kennedy Dean, *Live a Praying Life Without Fear* [10]

Dream a Little . . .

What do you want to be true about yourself when your life is over? What would you like to do for the Lord if you could accomplish anything? What weakness do you wish God could turn into a strength?

Dream a Little . . .

Your best decisions aren't made when you're afraid of dying but when you're committed to living.

—Erwin McManus[11]

Pray the Scripture

Lord Jesus,

I'm praying Your word by faith! A day is coming when I will boldly declare that I waited for You to help me, and You heard my cry. You lifted me out of the pit of despair, out of the mud and mire, and You set my feet on solid ground. You steadied me as I walked along. You have given me a new song to sing. You have performed such wonders in my life that many are amazed and learning to put their trust in You. May my whole life be an example of Your goodness and kindness. Thank you for redeeming my story! Amen.

Psalm 40:1–3, paraphrased and personalized

Soul Care for the Battle

From Where I Stand

Current Battles

- Most pressing: ....
  ....
  ....

- Most concerning: ....
  ....
  ....

- Background noise but bothersome: ....
  ....
  ....

Faith Perspective in This Moment

0—	5—	10—
Discouraged/ Hopeless	Stressed but Okay	Fired Up and Faith Filled

Thoughts I Have on Repeat

I'm Listening, Lord

When I quiet my heart, here's what I sense God saying to me . . .

I'm Listening, Lord

When I quiet my heart, here's what I sense God saying to me . . .

Eternity with Jesus will take our breath away. Unhindered intimacy with God. Abounding *joy* with no enemy opposition. Fellowship with our brothers and sisters as we share our awe-filled stories of how God intervened in our lives. *Together*, we'll marvel as we learn about all He provided and all He prevented, and we'll love Him even more than we did before. Jesus' desire to remember our faith-filled deeds and *reward* us for them will leave us utterly stunned.

—*Strong in Battle*, p. 27

Pray the Scripture

Write out this passage in a personalized and prayerful way.

> *Why am I discouraged?*
> *Why is my heart so sad?*
> *I will put my hope in God!*
> *I will praise him again—my Savior and my God!*
>
> Psalm 43:5

....

....

....

....

....

....

....

....

....

....

....

....

Holy Lament

We are Loved.

Jesus is more than we thought, hoped, or *imagined*. His wildness is a source of wonder, not of worry. His righteousness is deeper than the oceans. His *goodness* is higher than the heavens. His *faithfulness* exceeds our comprehension. So what does that make us? **Loved.** Who are we? **Christ's beloved.** We are *loved* when making bold proclamations near cool waters under sunny skies. We are loved when asking sincere questions in dark cells and darker times. We are *loved*.

—Dr. Alicia Britt Chole,
40 Days of Decrease[12]

Holy Lament

Write out your prayer of lament to God.

Holy Lament

Write out your prayer of lament to God.

Things I Love about My Life

Blessings in My Battle

Taking Thoughts Captive

Don't worry about anything; instead, pray about *everything*. Tell God what you need and thank him for all he has done. Then you will experience God's *peace*, which exceeds anything we can *understand*. His peace will guard your hearts and minds as you live in Christ Jesus.

Philippians 4:6–7

Self compassion helps build resilience, the internal flexibility to rebound and *recover* from painful, disappointing, and devasting times. . . . People who are self-critical and depressed do not *rebound* well from the difficulties of life; instead, they tend to be very self-focused as they try to *survive* their depression, anxiety, and the bully beating them up on the inside.

—Kim Fredrickson, *The Power of Positive Self-Talk*[13]

Thoughts That Don't Belong in My Brain

Do you lean more toward self-compassion or self-criticism? Do you say things to yourself that you'd never imagine saying to someone else? What does your inner critic say to you?

Thoughts about God

*We're strong in battle when we remember that
we're tethered to a strong and good God.*

Today, I praise You because You are . . .

_____

_____

_____

_____

_____

Today, I'm grateful for . . .

_____

_____

_____

_____

_____

_____

A Faith Perspective

If you've gone around this mountain one too many times and still can't seem to get a breakthrough, I'd suggest trying something new. Read books on the love of God. Memorize whole passages on God's love and compassion and pray them constantly. Keep a thankfulness journal. Ask God to show you if there's a core belief in you that has become an obstacle for you.

—Susie Larson, *Fully Alive:*
Learning to Flourish—Mind, Body & Spirit[14]

I Have Seen His Goodness

His goodness . . .

His beauty . . .

His provision . . .

His intervention . . .

> To live a fully blessed life, we must quit reading the Bible as a rule book and start reading it as a revelation of Christ and who we are in Him.
>
> —Alan Wright[15]

Reflective Questions / Journal Prompts

How has this battle taken a toll on my soul?

....

....

....

....

In what ways have I neglected self-care?

....

....

....

....

What can I do today to nourish my soul?

....

....

....

....

Healthy Choices I Made Today

Every step toward healing and wholeness matters.

I love you, LORD;
    you are my strength.
The LORD is my rock, my fortress, and my savior;
    my God is my rock, in whom I find protection.
He is my shield, the power that saves me,
    and my place of safety.
I called on the LORD, who is worthy of praise,
    and he saved me from my enemies.

The ropes of death entangled me;
    floods of destruction swept over me.
The grave wrapped its ropes around me;
    death laid a trap in my path.
But in my distress I cried out to the LORD;
    yes, I prayed to my God for help.
He heard me from his sanctuary;
    my cry to him reached his ears.

Psalm 18:1–6

Space for Reflection

I am going to be okay.

This week:

- [ ] Purposefully *tackle* one task that you've been putting off.
- [ ] Graciously take one commitment off your *calendar* that you know is not good for you.
- [ ] Boldly ask a *friend* (or friends) to join you for dinner.
- [ ] Creatively *cook* a meal that requires more preparation than you're used to,
- [ ] *Light* a few candles,
- [ ] Take some deep *breaths*,

AND *enjoy* . . .

Fully Alive Moment

Write about a time recently when you were most fully alive, when you felt like the best version of yourself.

Fully Alive Moment

Write about a time/memory when you were most fully alive, when you felt like the best version of yourself.

_____

_____

_____

_____

_____

_____

_____

_____

_____

_____

_____

Grace to you and peace from God our Father and the Lord Jesus Christ. I thank my God upon every remembrance of you.

Philippians 1:2–3 NKJV

Read through your memory and answer the following questions.

Precious Memories . .

What were you wearing? What might that outfit say about you?

....

....

....

....

What about that memory made you happy?

....

....

....

....

What senses were most awakened in that memory (e.g., what you tasted, touched, felt, heard, saw)?

....

....

....

....

Precious Memories . . .

What does this memory say about you?

How is this memory speaking to you even now?

Precious Memories . . .

What if this memory offers you insights into the ways God wants to restore you? With the framework of this memory in mind, write down what restoration might look like for you.

Take a moment and thank God for the nuances of this precious memory He's given you.

The Art of Remembering . . .

Becoming the *beloved* is pulling the truth revealed to me from *above* down into the ordinariness of what I am, in fact, thinking of, talking about and *doing* from hour to hour.

—Henri Nouwen[16]

Pray the Scripture

Write out this passage in a personalized and prayerful way.

Now all glory to God, who is able to keep you from fall-ing away and will bring you with great joy into his glorious presence without a single fault. All glory to him who alone is God, our Savior through Jesus Christ our Lord. All glory, majesty, power, and authority are his before all time, and in the present, and beyond all time! Amen.

Jude 1:24–25

....

....

....

....

....

....

....

....

....

....

....

....

Make a Memory This Week . . .

Did you know that anticipating good things is nourishment for your brain and very healing to your body?

Some fun things I could do this week . . .

My plan . . .

Why I look forward to this event . . .

Things I Love about My Life

Expectations versus Expectancy

Expectations often keep us from embracing wide-eyed, holy expectancy. What expectations have found their way into your heart? In what ways are you living with wide-eyed, holy expectancy?

Taste and see that the Lord is
    good.
Oh, the *joys* of those who take
    refuge in him!
Fear the Lord, you his *godly*
    people,
for those who *fear* him will
    have all they need.

Psalm 34:8–9

Time for Some Battle Inventory[17]

What do you know about God now that you didn't know prior to this trial?

_____

_____

_____

_____

_____

_____

How has your battle impacted your perspective of others?

_____

_____

_____

_____

_____

_____

_____

Battle Inventory

What biblical truths do you need right now (that maybe you forgot)?

....

....

....

....

....

....

....

What have been some of the more defining moments of your battle?

....

....

....

....

....

....

....

Battle Inventory

What in you still needs healing?

_____

_____

_____

_____

_____

_____

_____

How are you better, stronger, or wiser because of this battle?

_____

_____

_____

_____

_____

_____

_____

Pray the Scripture

Lord Jesus,

You have been so faithful, and You always will be. Help me to trust You with my whole heart. I know I only see in part, so I refuse to rely on my own understanding. I know I have the capacity to reason myself right out of obedience. So I lean wholeheartedly on You, trusting You to fill every gap and establish every step. Though You give wisdom to Your children, I must admit that I don't know what I don't know. I'm not wise in my own eyes. I honor You as Lord. I shun evil. I trust You to keep me safe. I believe You will bring healing to my body and strength to my frame. You are all I need, Lord, and I have You. How blessed am I! Thank You. With all my heart, thank You. Amen.

Proverbs 3:5–8, paraphrased and personalized

Encouraging Voices That Keep Me Grounded

Who is speaking into your life right now?
Friends, mentors, authors, pastors, family members?

I'm Listening, Lord

When I quiet my heart, here's what I sense God saying to me . . .

You are a *warrior* in the making. Ask God to show you your place on the wall. Raise your *shield* against enemy fire, not just for yourself but for the sake of those in *bondage* to the enemy's lies. What enemy scheme might fall apart because you *dared* to stand in the gap and pray?

———

—*Strong in Battle,* p. 53

Holy Lament

Have mercy on me, O God, have mercy!
  I look to you for protection.
I will hide beneath the shadow of your wings
  until the danger passes by.
I cry out to God Most High,
  to God who will fulfill his purpose for me.
He will send help from heaven to rescue me,
  disgracing those who hound me.   Interlude
  My God will send forth his unfailing love and faithfulness.

Psalm 57:1–3

Most of us go through life bleeding under our armor. It's good to give sacred time and space to pour out our hearts to God. Give yourself that gift today. Tell Him what's on your heart, how you feel about the battle, and how you long for Him to move.

....

....

....

....

....

....

....

....

Holy Lament

Write out your prayer of lament to God.

Things I Love about My Life

God Is Always Up to Something New

God is moving in your midst. Can you see it?
Sense it? Write down your thoughts.

For I am about to do something new.
See, I have already begun! Do you not see it?
I will make a pathway through the wilderness.
I will create rivers in the dry wasteland.

Isaiah 43:19

And the *Holy Spirit* helps us in our weakness. For example, we don't know what God wants us to pray for. But the Holy Spirit prays for us with groanings that cannot be *expressed* in words. And the Father who knows all hearts knows what the Spirit is saying, for the Spirit pleads for us believers in *harmony* with God's own will. And we know that God causes everything to work together for the good of those who *love* God and are called according to his purpose for them.

—Romans 8:26–28

God never said that the *journey*
would be easy, but he did say that
the *arrival* would be worthwhile.

———

—Max Lucado,
In the Eye of the Storm[18]

Thoughts That Don't Belong in My Brain

When we're not careful, we can too easily fall into grumbling and complaining about things that don't really matter that much, when in fact, we're more blessed than we know. What grumbly attitudes have found their way into your thoughts and heart?

Repentance

Lord, forgive me . . .

For these gifts I've taken for granted . . .

....

....

....

....

For blaming You for my troubles . . .

....

....

....

....

For my default ways of handling stress . . .

....

....

....

....

Repentance

Lord, forgive me . . .

For harboring unforgiveness in my heart . . .

For the unkind thoughts I've had toward others . . .

For the negative ways I've allowed my battles to impact me . . .

Thoughts about God

*We're strong in battle when we remember that
we're tethered to a strong and good God.*

Today, I praise You because You are . . .

_____

_____

_____

_____

_____

_____

Today, I'm grateful for . . .

_____

_____

_____

_____

_____

_____

Soul Care for the Battle

A Faith Perspective

Our greatest *ministry* will occur after we're dead—that is, after we're in heaven. We'll leave behind all the *work* we've done, the tasks we've completed, the *words* we've said and written, the people we've touched, the causes we've supported, the lives we've changed, the children we've raised, the churches we've sustained, the missionaries we've sent, and the funds we've invested in the *Kingdom*. It all has a ripple effect that expands until Christ returns.

—Dr. Robert Morgan,
The Jordan River Rules[19]

A Faith Perspective

Though we can't earn God's love or perform our way to salvation (praise God!), we can grow in our capacity to know God's love and provision in a way that changes us and changes the world through us. Expand on each of the following sentences:

I want to grow in the way that I live:

....

....

I want to grow in the ways that I give:

....

....

I want to grow in the words that I say:

....

....

I want to grow in the way that I pray:

....

....

Sorting through Your Disappointments

God will one day redeem our story in a way that overwhelms us with His goodness. His attention to detail and fierce love for us will leave us breathless with awe and wonder. But in the meantime, hurts and losses will happen. In what ways has your life not turned out the way you'd hoped? Which disappointments still sting for you?

Sorting through Your Disappointments

What does this disappointment say *to* you that you sense is not true?

....

....

....

What does this disappointment say *about* you that you sense is not true?

....

....

....

What does this disappointment say *to* you *about* God that is not true?[20]

....

....

....

> He will wipe every tear from their eyes, and there will be no more death or sorrow or crying or pain. All these things are gone forever.
>
> Revelation 21:4

The body tells its story in *stillness*.
When we are physically active,
we focus on the *motion* without
sensing the conversation going
on inside of us. In stillness, we
can recognize when *movement*
is no longer serving us well.

—Dr. Saundra Dalton-Smith,
Sacred Rest[21]

I Need Rest

In what ways have you neglected self-care? Sleep? Downtime? Time away from screens? Write about the kinds of rest you need and plan to rest.

I Need Rest

When you consider your areas of fatigue (physical, mental, emotional, etc.), how might you trust God more going forward than you've trusted Him up to this point? Write out your thoughts.

_____

_____

_____

_____

_____

_____

_____

_____

_____

_____

_____

> God is within her, she will not fall; God will help her at break of day.
>
> Psalm 46:5 NIV

Those who live in the *shelter* of
the Most High
will find *rest* in the shadow of
the Almighty.
This I declare about the Lord:
He alone is my *refuge*, my place
of safety;
he is my God, and I *trust*
him.

—Psalm 91:1–2

Things I Love about My Life

I Have Seen His Goodness

His goodness . . .

....

....

His beauty . . .

....

....

His provision . . .

....

....

His intervention . . .

....

....

> In prayer, I thank God for the beauty that's all around me. This is freeing, relaxing, and it returns me to the path of thankfulness toward God.
>
> —Gary Thomas, *The Glorious Pursuit*[22]

Reflective Questions / Journal Prompts

How has this battle taken a toll on my soul?

In what ways have I neglected self-care?

What can I do today to nourish to my soul?

Healthy Choices I Made Today

Every step toward healing and wholeness matters.

Soul Care for the Battle

Restore our fortunes, LORD,
   as streams *renew* the desert.
Those who plant in tears
   will harvest with shouts of *joy*.
They weep as they go to plant
   their seed,
   but they *sing* as they return
   with the harvest.

———

—Psalm 126:4–6

Space for Reflection

I am going to be okay.

☐ Grab a good *book*.

☐ Go to *bed* early.

☐ Take a few slow, deep *breaths*.

☐ *Thank* God for your pillow,
your blankets, and your bed.

☐ Ponder the *ways* you experi-
enced His goodness today.

☐ Read, smile, *enjoy*,

AND *rest*.

Me Time

Describe the kind of day that would replenish your soul.

Soul Care for the Battle

If we're not careful, our battles will make us *selfish*. And while it's important to tend to the matters of the *soul*, it's equally important to remember that God intends to reach the world *through* us.

Help Someone in Need

Who can you help today? How can you help today?

Picture, if you can, Jesus walking right into the middle of your circumstance and passionately imploring you, I want you to *dream* here. I want you to *feast* here. I want you to increase, not decrease here. I want you to be a blessing to those around you. I am doing a *new* thing. It won't always be this way. You don't see it clearly now, but will you trust me? Soon, and very soon, you will see the new thing I'm about to do for you. *Guard* your heart here . . . and remember what's *true* here, even when it doesn't feel true.

—Susie Larson, *Fully Alive*[23]

Praying for Others

What national or global issue most concerns you?
Write out your prayer and ask God to intervene.

A Healed You

Imagine yourself even a month from now.
What might a more healed you look like?

Blessed Is the One Who Trusts

For the LORD God is a sun and shield;
    the LORD bestows favor and honor;
no good thing does he withhold
    from those whose walk is blameless.

LORD Almighty,
    Blessed is the one who trusts in you.

Psalm 84:11–12 NIV

I Have Seen His Goodness

He provided . . .

He prevented . . .

He intervened . . .

He delivered . . .

The Ways He Loves Me

Pause and ponder the countless ways God has shown you that He loves you. Write down your thoughts.

Make a Memory This Week . . .

Anticipating good things is nourishment for your brain and very healing to your body.

Some fun things I could do this week . . .

My plan . . .

Why I look forward to this event . . .

The Memories I Made This Week

Memories I made this week that I didn't expect . . .

_____

_____

_____

_____

Memories I made that I intentionally pursued . . .

_____

_____

_____

_____

Ways that I'm growing when it comes to expectations versus expectancy . . .

_____

_____

_____

_____

Sing at the top of your lungs.
Laugh from the tips of your toes.

Celebrate even the smallest wins.

Tell your loved ones how
you feel about them.

Remind your soul that
God has been good.

And He'll be
GOOD AGAIN.

Healthy Choices I Made Today

Every step toward healing and wholeness matters.

Faith Declaration

Which part of this declaration does your soul need most?

As a citizen of the heavenly kingdom,
An heir of God and joint-heir with Christ,
Filled with the Spirit of the Living God,
I SPEAK WITH PRECISION,
I PRAY WITH POWER,
I walk in authority.
I am anointed and appointed,
Blessed and beloved,
Bold and brave,
Called and courageous,
Because I know God is with me.
I will triumph over my enemy,
And I will stand with Jesus on that final day.

—*Strong in Battle*, p. 147

Faith Declaration

Take the statements that most resonated with you from the previous page and write out your own personalized faith declaration. Find some Scripture to support your declaration.

Pray the Scripture

Precious Father,

I bless Your name with my whole heart! May I never forget the good things You've done for me; the marvelous things You do for me! You forgive all of my sins, heal all of my diseases, ransom my life from the pit, crown me with loving compassion; You satisfy my heart's desires with good things and my youth is renewed like the eagle's. How can I ever thank You enough for who You are and all You've done? My heart trust in You! My soul waits for You! In Jesus' matchless name, I pray. Amen.

Psalm 103:1–4, paraphrased and personalized

From Where I Stand

Current Battles

- Most pressing: ....

  ....

- Most concerning: ....

  ....

- Background noise but bothersome: ....

  ....

Faith Perspective in This Moment

0—
Discouraged/
Hopeless

5—
Stressed
but Okay

10—
Fired Up
and Faith Filled

Thoughts I Have on Repeat (healthy and unhealthy)

....

....

....

"For I know the *plans* I have
for you," declares the Lord,
"plans to *prosper* you
and not to harm you,
plans to give you
hope and a *future*."

—Jeremiah 29:11 NIV

Thoughts That Don't Belong in My Brain

Retraining My Brain

How do your dreams and doubts conflict? In other words, are there dreams in your heart that are repeatedly doused by your doubts? Write down your thoughts.

Thoughts That Don't Belong in My Brain

Retraining My Brain

*What's a more redemptive way to think
about your God-given dreams?*

I'm Listening, Lord

When I quiet my heart, here's what I sense God saying to me . . .

There's truly *no limit* to what God will do through a life humbly, wholly devoted to Him. He's looking for *saints* today who are willing to rise this hour and believe Him to be the God He declares Himself to be! When God searches the world over to find *faith* in the hearts of men, may He find holy, humble, *powerful* faith in us.

—*Strong in Battle*, p. 70

What Are You Afraid Of?

Write out your thoughts.

When You Can't Hear What God Is Saying,
Remember What He's Already Said

What has the Lord said to you in the past regarding your fears?
What promises has He made? What challenges has He issued?

How do we know if our battles
have *served* us well?
We will emerge from them leaning
on the arm of our *Beloved*.

—*Strong in Battle*, p. 82

Pray the Scripture

Write out this passage in a prayerful, personalized way.

The LORD is my light and my salvation—
whom shall, I fear?
The LORD is the stronghold of my life—
of whom shall I be afraid?

Psalm 27:1 NIV

....

....

....

....

....

....

....

....

....

....

....

....

....

Things I Love about My Life

Turn the Table on the Enemy

How do we turn the table on the enemy of our soul?
We trust God even when He seems silent.
We forgive those who don't even
know they need forgiveness.
We love others even though it costs us.
We've learned to be ruthless with the
enemy, yet kind to ourselves.
We know God's Word like we've never known before.
We pray with more power and consistency.
We walk in greater boldness and courage.
We're more focused on God's goodness
than the devil's badness.

I'm Listening, Lord

When I quiet my heart, here's what I sense God saying to me . . .

Pray the Scripture

Write out this passage in a personalized and prayerful way.

One thing I ask from the LORD,
*   this only do I seek:*
that I may dwell in the house of the LORD
*   all the days of my life,*
to gaze on the beauty of the LORD
*   and to seek him in his temple.*
For in the day of trouble
*   he will keep me safe in his dwelling;*
he will hide me in the shelter of his sacred tent
*   and set me high upon a rock.*

Psalm 27:4–5 NIV

Dream a Little . . .

What are you believing God for right now? In what ways has He confirmed His promises to you?

Dream a Little . . .

Jesus loves you. He loves your faith. He loves your
heart. He loves your story. Lean in and trust Him.

What Do You Know?

God has spoken to you in different ways throughout your battle. Just so you don't forget, write down the different ways He has confirmed His presence, His voice, and His direction in your life.

Stories and passages from Scripture that I returned to, time and time again:

Inner promptings and insights from the Holy Spirit:

Songs that have really ministered to my soul:

What Do You Know?

Looking back over your season of battle, how has God confirmed His presence and provision to you?

Friends who have spoken truth and encouragement to my heart (detail who they are and what they said):

....

....

....

....

Circumstances that caused me to pause and pay attention:

....

....

....

....

Books I read that helped me to better understand my struggle:

....

....

....

....

What Do You Know?

What advice do you have for someone who's right now where you were months ago?

What Do You Know?

Write a letter to your future self.
How do you want to encourage her?

What Do You Know?

Write out a prayer to God, thanking Him for His goodness and faithfulness in your life.

Strongholds are broken. Captives set *free*. The lost are found. You have work to do. You're recovering your roar. You refuse to be constantly kicked around by your enemy. You suddenly know and *believe* that this King you serve is far more powerful than you once thought. This means you now have the *divine* capacity to be mighty in battle.

—*Strong in Battle*, p. 139

Thank You, Jesus!

Write out a prayer thanking Jesus for His faithfulness to you.

NOTES

1. Jennie Allen, *Get Out of Your Head: Stopping the Spiral of Toxic Thoughts* (Colorado Springs, CO: Waterbrook, 2020), 127.

2. John Eldredge, *All Things New: Heaven, Earth, and the Restoration of Everything You Love* (Nashville, TN: Nelson Books, 2017), 9.

3. Casey Tygrett, *As I Recall: Discovering the Place of Memories in Our Spiritual Life* (Downers Grove, IL: IVP Books, 2019), 30.

4. Louie Giglio, *Don't Give the Enemy a Seat at Your Table* (Nashville, TN: W Publishing, 2021), 80.

5. Sharon Jaynes, *When You Don't Like Your Story: What If Your Worst Chapters Could Become Your Greatest Victories?* (Nashville, TN: Nelson Books, 2021), 2.

6. Susie Larson, *Fully Alive: Learning to Flourish—Mind, Body & Spirit* (Bloomington, MN: Bethany House Publishers, 2018), 11, 79, 165, 172.

7. Casey Tygrett, *As I Recall*, 48.

8. Lysa TerKeurst, Facebook, October 27, 2014. https://m.facebook.com /OfficialLysa/posts/today-no-matter-what-youre-going-through-backtrack-and -remember-all-the-places-w/10152403547522694/.

9. Francis Frangipane, *The Stronghold of God* (Lake Mary, FL: Charisma House, 1998), viii.

10. Jennifer Kennedy Dean, *Live a Praying Life Without Fear: Let Faith Tame Your Worries* (Birmingham, AL: New Hope Publishers, 2016), 84.

11. Erwin McManus, as quoted in Stephen Arterburn, *100 Days to Freedom from Fear and Anxiety* (Peabody, MA: Aspire Press, 2021), 17.

12. Alicia Britt Chole, *40 Days of Decrease: A Different Kind of Hunger. A Different Kind of Fast*. (Nashville, TN: W Publishing, 2016), 22, emphasis mine.

13. Kim Fredrickson, *The Power of Positive Self-Talk* (Grand Rapids, MI: Revell, 2015), 21, 22.

14. Susie Larson, *Fully Alive*, 134.

15. Alan Wright, *The Power to Bless: How to Speak Life and Empower the People You Love* (Grand Rapids, MI: Baker Books, 2021), 66.

16. Henri J.M. Nouwen, *Life of the Beloved: Spiritual Living in a Secular World* (New York: Crossroad, 1992), 46.

17. The questions in this section are adapted from those found in *Strong in Battle*, page 83.

18. Max Lucado, *In the Eye of the Storm: Jesus Knows How You Feel* (Nashville, TN: Thomas Nelson, 1991), 84.

19. Dr. Robert Morgan, *The Jordan River Rules: 10 God-Given Strategies for Moving Forward* (Nashville, TN: Robert J. Morgan, 2021), 82.

20. Questions adapted from those in my book *Your Powerful Prayers: Reaching the Heart of God with a Bold and Humble Faith* (Bloomington, MN: Bethany House Publishers, 2016), 43.

21. Dr. Saundra Dalton-Smith, MD, *Sacred Rest: Recover Your Life, Renew Your Energy, Restore Your Sanity* (New York, NY: Faith Words, 2017), 33.

22. Gary Thomas, *The Glorious Pursuit: Becoming Who God Created Us to Be* (Colorado Springs, CO: NavPress, 1998, 2020), 165.

23. Susie Larson, *Fully Alive,* 153.

Susie Larson is a national speaker, bestselling author, and the host of the daily talk show *Susie Larson Live*, heard on the Faith Radio Network. Susie's podcast has over 3.5 million downloads. Susie has written nineteen books and many articles. She's been a guest on *Focus on the Family*, the *Life Today* show, and *Family Life Today*, as well as many other media outlets. Twice voted a top-ten finalist for the John C. Maxwell Transformational Leadership Award, she is also a veteran of the fitness field. Susie has been married to her dear husband, Kevin, since 1985, and together they have three wonderful sons, three beautiful daughters-in-law, three beautiful grandchildren, and one adorable pit bull named Memphis. Susie's passion is to see people everywhere awakened to the value of their soul, the depth of God's love, and the height of their calling in Christ Jesus.

More from Susie Larson

In this beautifully designed collection of 90 blessings—for both mother and child—Susie Larson provides hope-filled biblical declarations so both of you can receive strength and nourishment for your souls. Speak life into your children, sowing God's Word into their hearts as you also are rooted in the promises of God.

May His Face Shine upon You

In the hurriedness of December, it's easy to forget about the sacredness of the season. What if you approached this Advent season with an open heart and room for God? *Prepare Him Room* invites you to give God sacred space in your holiday season and gives you time to ponder the miracle of Christ within you and respond to His astonishing work in your life.

Prepare Him Room

Everything God asks of us is for our good and His glory. But that doesn't mean life is easy, and sometimes we need to be reminded of God's power over all we face. In this inspiring devotional, Susie Larson offers 365 days' worth of opportunities for you to strengthen your walk in faith while finding a new level of freedom and redemption.

Prevail

⬥ BETHANYHOUSE

 Stay up to date on your favorite books and authors with our free e-newsletters. Sign up today at bethanyhouse.com.

 facebook.com/BHPnonfiction

 @bethany_house

 @bethany_house_nonfiction

You May Also Like . . .

What you believe about God and your place in His Kingdom has everything to do with how you'll fare in the battles of this life. In these pages, Susie Larson shares how you can gain victory in all the hardships and obstacles you face in this life. As you rely on God, you will discover greater discernment, power, and authority, and arise victorious.

Strong in Battle

BETHANYHOUSE